GW01017932

Sheriff and O
in the Global Village

◆

DAN PLESCH

MENARD PRESS

2002

Menard Press acknowledges with gratitude the support
of the Joseph Rowntree Reform Trust Limited

Menard Press would also like to thank
Antony Gray, Rosemary Gray and
Nathaniel Rudolf for their help.

The author thanks Menard Press for its invitation
to join the distinguished ranks of Menard pamphleteers.
He would also like to thank Martin Butcher, Dr Lindsay Forbes,
Dr Mike McGinty and Otfried Nassauer.
Any errors that escaped them are the author's own.

ISBN: 1 874320 30 6

Typography and design: Antony Gray

UK and Worldwide distribution and representation
(except North America)
Central Books/Troika
99 Wallis Road, Hackney Wick, London E9 5LN
Tel: 020-8986 4854   Fax: 020-8533 5821
E-mail for private customers: mo@centralbooks.com
E-mail for trade: orders@centralbooks.com

North America distribution
Small Press Distribution Inc.
1341 Seventh Street, Berkeley, CA 94710, USA
Books can be ordered via their website:
spdbooks.org

Menard Press
8 The Oaks, Woodside Avenue, London N12 8AR
Tel/fax: 020-8446 5571

Printed and bound in Great Britain by
Alden Press, Oxford

Contents

Introduction

The easy victory over the Taliban and the absence of more major attacks could make us believe that September 11th was a one-off and we can now relax. On the other hand, such devastating attacks only need occur every few years for the attackers to keep the upper hand and retain the initiative. This new form of warfare remains a major threat.

Before September 11th, globalisation and the threat from weapons of mass destruction were the greatest challenges the world faced. Now we must add the problem of global terrorism. A successful counter-terrorism strategy requires international co-operation and economic development. The main problem of globalisation is the oligarchy of economic and military interests using new technologies to establish global supremacy. Weapons of mass destruction are regarded as fundamental sources of power by some countries. The rivalry over these weapons prevents a collective effort aimed at stopping terrorists from obtaining them or at eliminating them altogether. These aspects of globalisation and weapons of mass destruction hinder a successful anti-terrorism strategy.

In this essay, I mainly avoid using the word terrorist. This is not because I have any sympathy with Bin Laden and his associates but because 'terrorist' is an emotive and unclear word. Some people have been members of terrorist groups and gone on to lead democratic nations. Members of the Irgun wing of the Zionist movement and parts of the South African ANC come to mind. Other people in and out of government have perpetrated terrible acts against civilians and neither deserved nor received political rehabilitation. More neutral words such as 'guerrilla' make things clearer. The problem is too serious to call people names.

All of the topics discussed deserve more detailed attention than the space allows. I have sought to avoid rehashing what is well known and to concentrate on the key policy issues. I have given rather more detailed attention to the problem of weapons of mass destruction than to other topics as the impact of their possession and use by either governments or terrorists is so great and because nowadays they are less well known than they were in say the 1980s. There are no recommendations for more weapons: they exist in superfluity and I consider that there is little need for any more. On the contrary, the need is to develop the non-military strategies that can reduce and remove the need for weapons.

A Global Guerrilla War

The events of September 11th were unprecedented. They highlighted the vulnerability of modern societies to violence by autonomous groups.

September 11th was the first successful attack by a guerrilla force on a major power in modern history. **It was the first time a Western power centre has been attacked by non-Westerners since the Ottoman Turks besieged Vienna in the seventeenth century.** The Japanese attack on Pearl Harbor only reached a far outpost of US power.

Most individual acts of what we have come to call terrorism have killed or held hostage a few dozen people with the objective of shock and news coverage. The attacks of September 11th included the psychological element but also physically destroyed centres of US power and were timed to hurt the US economy. The US has put the economic cost at $639 billion. The scale of the attacks on centres of power makes it appropriate to call them strategic.

Notes from the Al Qaeda classrooms of Afghanistan reveal an imaginative range of other targets and weapons. No one can be sure how many more attacks are planned. Future attacks could use nuclear,[1] chemical or biological weapons.[2] Al Qaeda operates globally. It has or had sections responsible for finance, weapons procurement, propaganda, recruitment, training and communications. The attacks were the culmination of other efforts over several years. Together they demonstrated the sophistication of planning and execution that would normally be associated with a developed state apparatus. Al Qaeda functions or functioned not only in the US but also in many parts of Europe, the Middle East and Asia. A quick survey of the websites of major newspapers shows how many countries the network is known publicly to operate in, and the wide variety of actions it has taken or might take in the future. No one can know how many other groups and governments will see this new form of warfare as a means of responding to Western and especially US military supremacy.

Several aspects of the current crisis make it analogous to a civil war: that it is taking place in a world which globalisation has shrunk and interconnected; the strategic nature of the attacks; that the attacks do not appear to be by a state and that some of the attackers come from within the societies attacked. The term a 'clash of civilisations' is the most common way of describing the potential global civil war, but the 'Islamic-Christian' issue is not what characterises the conflict as global civil war.

In olden days, attacks by guerrillas on the economic and technical structure of society could not produce catastrophe. Societies were far more decentralised and mass-destruction weapons were not available.

The period after 1945 saw the world change with the invention of satellite TV links and missiles that could cross the world in thirty minutes. These and other advances gave rise to the term 'global village'. Today the world has shrunk still further. The Internet, the mobile phone and the mingling of peoples have created a world in which we experience instant communication and cultural variety. **The global village has shrunk to Earth Avenue.**

The methods used in the attacks on the World Trade Center were a way of hitting back for people without large-scale technology. They are equivalent to throwing rocks through the front windows of the rich, even of torching the mansion. In this small space, commandos and cruise missiles act as an international riot squad.

The US-led response to the attacks of September 11th

The 'war on terrorism' has mainly been a traditional military expedition against Afghanistan, using bombs and cash to topple a corrupt and despotic regime. Significantly, though, the attacks were arranged to reduce civilian casualties out of concern for the innocent and in order to keep international support for the action. In the age of imperialism, inflicting civilian casualties was an important punitive objective.

So far the objective of capturing Usama Bin Laden and the top leaders of his group and of the Taliban regime has not been achieved. Many Al Qaeda and Taliban have been killed and some captured. Many have escaped and an unknown number remain in other countries. The attack on Afghanistan has destroyed the mass training camps but it may only have brought the illusion of victory as effective fighters remain at large. Ten to twenty thousand men were trained in Afghanistan, but not more than five thousand appear to have been killed or captured till now.

The US strategy of employing Afghan allies has been effective in reducing the perception in the Islamic world that the conflict is between the West and Islam. It has also reduced US casualties. However, there has been a serious cost.

As the US tightens its grip on Afghanistan, so its enemies seem to slip through its fingers like sand. There were not enough US troops in the mountains to create a line to prevent the leaders of Al Qaeda vanishing in the dark and the blizzards, bribing their way to safety when necessary.

US commentators laud the victory of their armed forces. Few, if any, dare to suggest that American reluctance to accept casualties has prolonged the 'war on terrorism'.

The US troops remain. The UK and its allies are creating a UN mandated stabilisation force in Kabul. Already their liberating role is at risk of being forgotten as they get caught up in the country's problems.

The commitment led by the UK to rebuild the country is gathering pace. Substantial sums have been committed by donor nations and, led by the Algerian diplomat Ambassador Brahimi, the UN effort will hopefully have learned lessons from poor administration in Cambodia and the Balkans. The war against opium production in Afghanistan will be the next major test of the international operation and the work of the UN Drug Programme will be crucial.[3]

Military history abounds with tales of an over-confident and superior enemy being drawn by the prospect of easy victory on to the ground of the enemy's choosing. The war in Afghanistan is not over yet and the potential for a confused guerrilla war remains. Even if the Afghan chapter of the conflict is closing, the US is already engaged in military operations in the Philippines and Colombia.

The US and other states remain vulnerable at home. Overstretched security forces across the US are approaching exhaustion after months of emergency duty. The defenders need to get it right all the time. Unfortunately, the defence appears far from sound. People are working hard in all the agencies, but the US has not had to think hard about this type of threat in the past and is inexperienced at the task. President Bush's principal action inside the US has been to create a presidential 'Office of Homeland Defense'. The White House National Security Council was too concerned with other nations' security to devote itself to the homeland. The new agency had to be created from scratch. The new office has no authority over other agencies' plans and budgets and has only a handful of staff of its own.

Recommended measure:
❑ **Homeland defence should concentrate on improving co-ordination between agencies**

The lack of a broader strategy

There is a military component to fighting terrorism but there is no military solution. The military contribution exists in abundance. Any effective solution requires tighter security and detection of the perpetrators and here intelligence is critical. It also requires a new effort to reduce our vulnerability to attack, but the central requirement is to create the political climate in which extremists are isolated both from their supporters and from those who might ignore their activities.

We need the best strategy to win this global guerrilla war. There is little sign in the US that key lessons of successful tactics have been adopted. In many civil wars over the last fifty years, the political battle has been the decisive factor in resolving the conflict. In Ireland, the 'troubles' lasted thirty years before the political process overrode the cycle of violence. In South Africa, Guatemala, El Salvador, Sri Lanka and the Basque country political action has been critical in limiting or resolving conflict. The message from Washington has almost exclusively concerned military action, with debate focusing on where the next war should be waged.

The development of globally effective political and economic anti-terrorist measures has not begun. A review of the principal issues that need to be tackled demonstrates this. The Israeli–Palestinian conflict is getting worse, the concerns of US allies over a range of arms control and environmental measures have not been positively reassessed, eliminating global poverty is not a US priority and the United States national security budget continues in much the same way as before. The emphasis is on expensive armaments to combat a non-existent high-tech competitor.

Non-military means of conducting foreign policy, such as disarmament, diplomacy, aid and even information, are still starved of support. The latest increase in the defence budget would be better spent in a broader effort aimed at conflict prevention. **The international equivalents of inner-city regeneration are neglected at the expense of more equipment for the riot squad.**

The US's European allies seem unable to do much better. They also neglect conflict prevention. Tony Blair's engagement of Iran and tours of the Middle East have run out of steam. In early 2002, the conflict between India and Pakistan was taking the attention of hard-pressed leaders away from the 'war on terrorism'.

Bush administration foreign policy

The Bush administration's policies are not an aberration but an acceleration of existing trends. There was already a heavily military foreign policy. International legal constraints were already being weakened. In contrast to security policy, US economic policy working through the world financial institutions puts ever-greater legal requirements on other countries to allow free access for corporations.

The prevailing US approach in world affairs is an unabashed pursuit of US interests buoyed by a supreme sense of self-confidence in American values and indeed in America's 'manifest destiny'. It is not so much a 'unilateralist' approach to world security as an anarchistic one. The dictionary definition of an anarchist is someone who does not accept the rule of law. In defence and security policy, the US sees little value these days in international law.

This political approach indulges Israel because it is the only democracy in the Middle East, maintains that Europeans are hopelessly irresolute and prone to accommodate dictatorships, and considers that treaties only serve to limit future action by the United States. From this perspective, America's democratic, economic and military values offer the world the best of futures. America's way is the best way not just for the United States but for the world as a whole. If anyone doubts this, it is argued, take a quick trip to any immigration office, full of people from all over the planet anxious to become Americans. As Tony Blair reminded us, where else could the son of Jamaican immigrants become first the nation's top general and then foreign minister in the most right-wing administration since the 1920s? It is the United States that won two world wars and the Cold War, has twice defended Muslim peoples in the Balkans and restored the sovereignty of Kuwait.

Many people, indeed many Americans, would dispute this version of history while still valuing the achievement that is the United States. They might say that the US, having been late for two world wars has seemed eager to be early for the third. It was not the arms race but structural decay and the dissidents in Eastern Europe that were decisive in the collapse of Communism. The Balkan conflicts were prolonged by the US until President Clinton and NATO could determine the outcome. It can be argued that we may come to see the 1990s as a little like the 1920s – a decade where the peace was squandered while the economy boomed.

One US Democrat has outlined a multilateral strategy with which the US could manage its global hegemony. This writer, Zbigniew

Brzezinski, who was President Carter's National Security Adviser, wrote in his work *The Grand Chessboard*:[4]

> For America, the chief geopolitical prize is Eurasia. Now a non-Eurasian power [the US] is pre-eminent in Eurasia – and America's global primacy is directly dependent on how long and how effectively its preponderance on the Eurasian continent is sustained.
>
> To put it in a terminology that harkens back to the more brutal age of ancient empires, the three grand imperatives of imperial geostrategy are to prevent collusion and maintain security dependence among the vassals, to keep tributaries pliant and protected, and to keep the barbarians from coming together.

Today we are faced with an administration in Washington that seems to share this analysis but is somewhat keener than Brzezinski to dispense solutions of its own making rather than work in concert with others.

The military basis for these approaches was established in the 1990s in the published US national strategy. The military objective is to maintain 'Full Spectrum Dominance'. This colourful phrase is much repeated in other documents such as the US military's Joint Staff document, 'Vision 2020'. This lays out plans for winning any conflict anywhere on earth, from guerrilla war to war in space. For US defence planners, the latest project is to establish dominance in space warfare and in missile wars. This is the so-called 'Star Wars' concept, which is discussed in more detail later.

Can the US and its allies rely on this approach to terrorism?

The current US approach does not have a track record of military success against terrorism despite the apparent victory in Afghanistan. Nor does it have the necessary ability to look at the world from the adversary's perspective.

It is a normal part of good human communication to try to see how others see us. In war, gaining such insight is indispensable, unless one is utterly confident of victory. On September 11th the US suffered an unprecedented blow and there should now be no such confidence. Unfortunately, the debate in the US on 'why do people hate us?' is cut short by accusations of appeasement or weak-minded liberalism. This can only give comfort to the guerrillas. Seeking to understand the other point of view does not mean that we have to like it. We do not have to sympathise in order to empathise.

In terms of the TV series *Star Trek*, we in the West see ourselves as a

'Federation' of benevolent, globalising, free-market democracies. 'They' see us as the Borg preaching that they must be assimilated, as we 'teach the world to sing in perfect harmony'. 'Suicide bombers' would in Western fiction be resistance heroes. 'Our' Christianity is a religion of compassion which to others has its own horrors such as the idea that babies are born sinful, not to mention the apparently cannibalistic ceremony of eating and drinking the flesh and blood of the messiah.

With the military approach to terrorism demonstrably ineffective, the threat has grown worse. Al Qaeda's attacks have become increasingly powerful over the years. Guerrillas forced the Israelis to withdraw from Southern Lebanon. Suicide attacks are becoming fashionable. In South America, the US 'Plan Colombia' does not appear to be reducing overall coca production. According to human rights groups, the US-supported paramilitaries often behave worse than the Marxist FARC guerrillas and are also drug traffickers. Armed groups have been very difficult to defeat even in cases where sophisticated long-term strategies of engagement have been followed, such as in the Basque region since the end of the Franco dictatorship or in the North of Ireland.

Al Qaeda is more ruthless and harder to defeat as it flits from place to place, arming itself from the global supermarket of weaponry and shielded by the sullen resentment of the affronted, the envious and the dispossessed. Military action which kills the innocent in the area attacked makes the survivors more sympathetic to the cause of the guerrillas. It is a well-known tactic of guerrillas to incite such attacks for just this reason. Where the action against the guerrillas also ignores democracy and other human rights the 'war on terrorism' becomes unjust and illegitimate.

The US does not see the need for a change of strategy. This is comparable to the inability of the British army to see that their red coats made easy targets when fighting the American revolutionaries in the 1770s and the Boer farmers of South Africa one hundred years later. We look at such blunders with disdain and believe ourselves to be superior. Nowadays it is our whole societies that are the easy targets, and our purchases of new fighter jets the equivalent of ordering fresh red coats – which were intimidating in their day.

Today our leaders seem as blind to great changes in the strategic environment as the British were in their red coats. Only when the might of the British Empire faced defeat in South Africa did it finally abandon red for khaki. No amount of new jargon such as 'asymmetric warfare' can substitute for a radical reassessment of threats and responses.

Recommended measure:

❑ **The vital security and enforcement element in combating terrorism should be subject to a far broader global strategy and not the other way around.**

Effective Global Security Strategies

Broader socio-economic strategies

A major political issue is the disproportionate power of the wealthy states in the world and the major corporations within them. In the US, corporations use their wealth to influence politics. Elections mostly hinge on how much cash the candidates have. Terrorism and social disorder thrive in poverty, especially if poverty is reinforced by injustice. Religious and cultural tensions are amplified by poverty. If the West Bank and Gaza were prosperous, the conflict in the area would be less intense.

'I defy you to agitate a man with a full stomach,' wrote William Cobbett the eighteenth-century English commentator. Today, after millions more words have been expended on the topic of poverty and social unrest, this adage is hard to improve upon. Certainly, Al Qaeda leaders are from the ranks of the well-fed, but the poor have been led by the disaffected middle classes since Robin Hood.

This point is still lost on many of those who take decisions on international security issues. There have been some positive changes of late. The Labour government in Britain has committed itself to working internationally to abolish poverty. The United States has a large aid programme in absolute terms and supports a charitable sector with significant tax breaks.

The need to address global poverty, however, has not made it on to the national security agenda. US national security strategy assumes that poverty in a huge swathe of the world stretching from Morocco to the Philippines and in parts of Latin America will continue for the foreseeable future. The US economic model tends to see poverty as a spur to enterprise, not something to be smothered in a welfare culture.

Recommended measure:
❑ **International development and aid policies should adopt the old medical principle: first, do no harm. Three 'harms' inflicted by the industrialised world that impede development are weapons transfers, high tariffs and debt repayments.**

In countless neighbourhoods and many entire societies, development is prevented by the misuse of firearms. The pioneering work of the International Action Network on Small Arms has put this issue on the agenda of most international agencies with help from the UK and other progressive governments. Insufficient political will has prevented codes of conduct and programmes of action becoming effective. For example, NATO has failed to implement its own policies for managing the mass of small arms littering Eastern Europe since the end of the Cold War. This is a source of supply for criminals and terrorists alike. Even less has been done about the trade in large weapons systems.

High tariffs by the EU, the US and other Western states on imports of food and clothing from poor states prevents these countries from benefiting from free trade. Some estimates put the loss of income at over $100 billion a year.

The problem of the indebtedness of developing states remains, despite some progress in debt rescheduling.

Aid that is delivered is mostly spent on products produced by the donor countries and is often simply a hidden form of domestic industrial subsidy. 'Aid' needs to assist more directly those for whom it is intended.

Unless we change our policies, we will find ourselves spending money on military intervention that could have been spent on prevention through a fair economic deal. By continuing policies that keep developing countries unstable, we help create situations that keep alive the Victorian idea of the White Man's Burden – the idea that we have a duty to civilise the barbarous in the developing world.

Curbing globalisation

The anti-globalisation movement is struggling to influence the corporate world. In principle, the problem is not globalisation, but oligarchy. A plate of spaghetti with tomato sauce combines Chinese noodles and South American tomatoes in the Italian kitchen. The fusing of cultures and ideas is not the problem. The heart of the problem is the concentration of power in a small group of corporations and the difficulty of creating any counterbalancing power base. Politicians justify oligopolisation by arguing that the decisions they make at the meetings of the World Trade Organisation and the G8 are democratic. But corporate interests continue to reduce the politicians' options. Politicians representing one patch of the planet are anxious not to give business an excuse to move next door.

A key demand of corporations is the deregulation of any measures that stand in their way. But the central driver in the success of capitalism is the government regulation that provides investors with immunity from the law. The very name 'public liability company' (PLC) stresses that investors may have the power and benefits of investment without being personally liable. Enron's executives can be prosecuted but not its shareholders.

Recommended measure:
❑ **Deregulation of investor immunity should be a major focus of the effort to make corporations accountable.**

Until the 1980s, there was some balance between the different interests in society. Regulations that favoured investors were balanced with trade union rights and limits on corporations. Over the last generation, these regulations have been greatly reduced but investor immunity has been left unchallenged.

Defenders of the deregulated system argue that without investor immunity there will be no investment, or that investment will go elsewhere. However, curbs on investor immunity could be traded for restoration of the regulation of corporations that used to ensure a more balanced power relationship in our societies. The issue of investor immunity can become a unifying and rallying demand with which to engage the corporate oligarchies at global negotiations.

Improving intelligence

Accurate information is essential to defeating terrorism. Information can be collected from open sources, by high-tech sources and from traditional spies.

A great deal of information can be obtained from open sources, such as newspapers, media broadcasts and the Internet but requires high-quality analysis not just by people with a simple ability in the relevant language but also a sufficient cultural understanding to assess the nuances of material.

A key tool of intelligence-gathering on nations has been satellite imaging that includes not just normal photography but atmospheric analysis to detect chemicals. In tackling guerrillas dispersed in cities these tools are useless. A great deal of material can be gathered by some states, especially the US and the UK, using satellites and land lines to listen to telecommunications. This Signals Intelligence or SIGINT is indispensable in the task of uncovering financial transactions. It is difficult for the intelligence agencies' computer equipment to keep up with the quantity of material to be surveyed and the quality of the encryption. Issues such as the privacy of the citizen from the state and its secret police forces and the intrusion of one nation's surveillance into the operations of another arise. The US–UK 'Echelon' programme for spying on telecommunications in Europe and elsewhere has attracted critical attention, including an investigation by the European Parliament.

The detailed on-the-ground process of criminal detection and spying is more important than the use of remote detection and communications monitoring in tracking guerrillas. This is sometimes referred to as 'human intelligence' or HUMINT.

The information needs to come from within individual law enforcement agencies in relevant countries and must be shared between states.

Intelligence co-operation

Most people assume that western countries already share information about terrorism. After all, terrorism has been a key issue in the communiqués of world leaders since the PLO began hijacking planes in the 1960s. But sharing is the exception, not the rule. In the aftermath of September 11th there have been numerous press reports of information in one country such as Germany, Spain, the UK or the US not having been shared with law-enforcement agencies in other states. The rush to share information after the event is a clear indication that this had not been done already, despite Al Qaeda's previous attacks. Some improvement has taken place in the short term, but senior officials in the US and in Europe remain concerned that this emergency co-operation is not even beginning to tackle the underlying problem.

In reality intelligence is often shared poorly between agencies of the same government. In Britain, the rivalry between MI5 and MI6, especially over Ireland, was well recognised but is now less marked. The controversial memoirs of ex-agents such as Peter Wright and David Shayler are as much concerned with incompetence and bureaucratic rivalries as alleged skullduggery.

In the US there are a number of massive organisations working on intelligence. They include the Central Intelligence Agency, the Federal Bureau of Investigation, the Defence Intelligence Agency, the National Reconnaissance Office, the National Security Agency, sections of the Armed Forces, the State Department, the Treasury and the Customs Service. Co-ordination between these organisations is notoriously poor.

The US–UK intelligence relationship is extended to a few other states – Australia, Canada and New Zealand. Even this network tends to be confined to intelligence drawn from high-tech tools such as satellites.

Failure to co-operate is a long-standing feature of the intelligence world. Commanders in the Gulf War noted how key information about the Iraqi army was withheld from the generals doing the fighting, so obsessed are the gatherers of intelligence with preserving their secrets. In NATO operations in the Balkans, intelligence is rarely shared between the nations involved and intelligence gathered by national armies is not given to the UN police command.

One long-serving member of the UK's intelligence community, Michael Herman, has written of the need for greater co-operation post September 11th. He commented that: 'In the longer term there is some incompatibility between seeking closer co-operation with foreign states and continuing to spy on them.'[5] A senior Western official dissuaded me from telephoning him with the words: 'I do not want a transcript of our chat handed to me by the Americans.' Rather more seriously, during the Dayton Peace Accord discussions at an airbase in the US, the British delegation was prevented from having its own communication system and was made to rely on the US and had to get clearance from the US before speaking to London.

Returning to our image of 'Earth Avenue', it is as if each building had its own laws and security team unconnected with those next door. In this environment the criminal is free to dodge from block to block, confident that the pieces will rarely be put together.

A one-nation, go-it-alone approach cannot hope to achieve adequate results. A multi-national, multi-agency approach is essential. In the short term the urgency of the threat has brought officials together as never before, but without the overall commitment to working together and respecting others' interests this intelligence co-operation is already proving to be fragile.

American perceptions of US–French co-operation are a useful example where, despite effective co-operation detailed in news reports, a close US ally is denigrated by opinion-leaders. Zacarais Moussaoui, the only member of the group that carried out the September 11th attacks so far charged by the US, has been accused on the basis of information supplied by France well in advance of the attacks. French intelligence also briefed the US on an attempt made in 1995 to crash an airliner into the Eiffel Tower. Nevertheless, France has been singled out for public ridicule by Charles Krauthammer, a leading US TV and newspaper pundit, in an article damning the relevance of multilateral engagement. To use the language of the Cold War, Mr Krauthammer's wilful ignorance makes him an unwitting aide of Usama Bin Laden.

The way ahead

The public in democracies expect a far more common-sense approach to sharing of operational intelligence on terrorist/guerrilla suspects and networks.

Recommended measures:

❏ **Concerning intelligence:**

Acceptance that multilateral co-operation is necessary for effective intelligence;

greater democratic accountability;

clear improvement in co-operation between agencies.

International law and order, the UN and democracy

Phrases like 'new international order' are sound bites used by world leaders at times of global crisis. At the end of the Cold War, George Bush Senior promised a 'New World Order', and similar language has been in use, especially by Tony Blair, since September 11th.

Over the last ten years there have been two opposite tendencies shaping international politics. The first has been a weakening of the UN and the international security system to allow US-led actions through NATO and 'Coalitions of the Willing', which are temporary coalitions of states prepared to carry out an intervention. US support for undemocratic regimes in the Middle East, Indonesia and South America threatens its international legitimacy.

In contrast there has been an effort led by pressure groups and aid agencies in conjunction with some governments (including at times the Clinton Administration) for international war crimes courts, for greater expectations of democratic values around the world and controls on armaments.

At present, the key problem we are facing is that the self-styled sheriff does not command the confidence of the global community. As a result, the 'posse' of allies mostly stays at home. The type of consensus that existed at the time of the Gulf War can be highly effective, but it relies on give and take.

International law and order and the role of the UN since September 11th

In the days following September 11th there was the question of whether the 'war on terrorism' was legally a war. This was followed by the issue of the legal basis of the military action against Afghanistan. The United States recognised that at this moment of peril it could not ignore the UN and submitted a letter to the Security Council citing a right of self-defence under Article 51 of the UN Charter. The UK followed suit, but did not follow the US in asserting a right to attack others subsequently identified as having been or intending to be involved in similar acts.

As the war unfolded a discussion began about what charges could be brought against the terrorists in what court. The Bush administration has developed the idea of using military tribunals sitting outside the United States. Many commentators have recommended the use of a UN war crimes tribunal or the nascent International Criminal Court to try the perpetrators of September 11th.

During the fighting in Afghanistan the willingness or otherwise of the US to take or accept prisoners became somewhat controversial. The legality of killing prisoners or killing people trying to surrender is questionable, though when people 'surrender' only to blow up their captors and themselves one can soon see that the legal issues are far from simple.

In the same period of late 2001, the US withdrew from two international agreements governing weapons of mass destruction. The first is the Anti-Ballistic Missile Treaty, which it will withdraw from on 13 June 2002. The second is on the creation of a verification system to enforce the abolition of biological weapons. The US also sought to prevent negotiations on this system ever taking place in the future.

What should be the role of international law in the 'war on terrorism' and other international affairs?

In Britain there is a breadth of agreement on the role of international law that may be surprising to some. In a recent review of the war, the Chief of Staff, Admiral Sir Michael Boyce, remarked that: 'Above all, what we do must be legal, or otherwise we jeopardise our legitimacy.' In similar vein Tony Benn remarked that the choice between a global law of the jungle and international law under the UN is the key issue for the new century.

Over the last decade however a view has grown in strength and reached a high point in the Bush administration that international law in the field of security is not in US interests. John Bolton, President Bush's new Under Secretary of State for Arms Control, told the US Senate that in his view, from a philosophical point of view, international law did not actually exist. Bush administration officials have made clear that they see no role for more treaties in controlling weapons of mass destruction. This policy is symptomatic of a widespread distaste among conservative Americans for any kind of legal constraint on US policy. From this viewpoint international law should simply be used when it is convenient to use it. This attitude is of course not confined to the US. Many governments and national traditions have played fast and loose with international law.

In the past in the US there has been a great tradition of international law. The US played a leading role in the creation of the United Nations and that body's Universal Declaration of Human Rights. In the period since 1945, the US has been at the forefront of creating legal frameworks to control armaments, including the nuclear Non-Proliferation Treaty.

A fair summary of the prevailing US view is that only the good guys (i.e. us) obey the law and that the bad guys cheat and get away with it. In short, international laws on security are for suckers. In any event, it is argued, US power is now so great that it does not need to trade off limitations on its power against those of other states.

This is not to say that people who support this perspective reject all forms of regulation. Their model is to export US practice, either directly by imposing laws on other countries or through US-led international groupings operating in secret, such as the 'Australia Group'. This tries to prevent export of materials for the construction of chemical weapons. A club of good people checking up on transfers of dangerous materials is useful, but it is no substitute for an agreement that brings in more and more countries such as Iran, which are seeking to change their role in world affairs.

These groupings permit transfers of weapons within the 'club'. Selling Trident and Cruise missiles to the UK is good, but to the developing world, bad. The 'club' approach perpetuates Western supremacy and invites competition.

The simplest way of seeing the limitations of the US go-it-alone approach to security policy is to envisage the world without international law. A policy that sets aside international law will create global anarchy. Historians call our present treaty arrangements the 'Westphalian system' from the German province where treaties were signed after the devastating wars of the seventeenth century.

If we abandon international law now, we face a return to the Middle Ages. As Otfried Nassauer has pointed out, an unravelling of international law threatens to tear apart the fabric of the European Union, as the premise of the Union is that states can make legal agreements with one another. There will be no internationally legitimate way of dealing with international terrorists. There will be no control over the corporate oligarchy. There is no justice in a future world run according to US regulations where other countries have no representation in US law making.

It is common to speak of the US as the 'world's policeman'. This is an inaccurate description. Police are accountable to legal authority, in effective democracies they are a positive force, in many other states they are an instrument of repression. Everywhere they represent the overall authority of the state. The US role is more that of a rent-a-cop, unwilling to respond to calls from the poor, all too ready to react when the interests of the well-off are at risk. When the US is persuaded to act in a somewhat altruistic fashion, then it makes it clear that it will determine the outcome. The role of the 'town council' at the United Nations HQ in New York is kept to a minimum.

A reason given by powerful countries for not using the UN is to avoid bargaining with countries they often do not agree with. But are the deals made to shore up the present approach any better? It is doubtful.

With international law under assault from both the world's major power and from international networks of guerrillas/terrorists it is necessary to reassess and affirm core values before advancing a pro-gramme of improvement.

As with the principles established at the Nuremberg trials, the United Nations involves a new approach in the long history of inter-national relations. Support for the UN as international legislature and police service is not universal. Although development in this area is slow, agreement can be achieved. A historical parallel shows us that a strong legal framework can be developed from disparate sources. US law has evolved from English Common Law over the last two centuries. English law itself evolved over centuries in contrast to the continental Napoleonic code constructed in the wake of the French Revolution. English law counts among its ancestors Roman law, Viking, Norman and Anglo-Saxon practices. The US characterises itself as a 'nation of laws' and is certainly a nation of lawyers. It should be the first to see the value of international law.

The task at a global level is to accelerate this evolution of international law. **The danger is that we are entering a period of renewed global anarchy welcomed both by a superpower that shrugs off constraint and by armed groups intent on destroying a globalized system which they find alien.**

The way ahead

Recommended measures:
- ❏ **Progress on legal controls on international security should be linked with legal agreements on trade.**
- ❏ **Interventions in sovereign states should have explicit UN mandates and the UN should have a strong role in managing operations to prevent them becoming a new form of imperialism.**
- ❏ **The International Criminal Court should be brought into force as soon as possible.**
- ❏ **The EU should initiate *ad hoc* international agreements with the developing world in preparation for the day when states that now reject them are ready to join in a UN sanctioned agreement.**
- ❏ **Democracy in international institutions should be increased. Nations should directly elect their representatives to the UN General Assembly.**

Global institutions are becoming weaker when it is clearer than ever that they need to be strengthened. A much more direct infusion of democratic power and legitimacy is needed. A start should be made at the UN where at present nations are represented by career bureaucrats. UN representatives should be elected directly. Such an arrangement would require adjustment to present constitutional arrangements in different countries. A number of commentators and politicians, such as the Foreign Office minister Peter Hain, have described how domestic and foreign policy have become indistinguishable. So far, however, our constitution has not adjusted to this. We should directly elect not just our representatives at the UN but at other international bodies such as NATO and the World Bank. In this way accountable politicians can represent us on a day-to-day basis, not just at summit time.

It is unlikely that the first elections will be held in Britain, Russia or the US, but if they were held in Ireland, South Africa or India, the legitimacy of the United Nations General Assembly would be greatly increased. Most proposals for UN reform can be blocked by powerful states, but directly electing members of the General Assembly is a measure any state can begin. We might ultimately see a global confederacy of sovereign states.

Reducing strategic vulnerability

Open, democratic, enjoyable societies will always be vulnerable. Large prominent buildings and advanced industries will remain juicy targets. As we are in a conflict that may last decades and in which the attackers wish to cripple our societies then these targets should be minimised.

Another key vulnerability in Western strategy stems from the construction of energy policy. Action in the Middle East is constrained by the imperative of ensuring a secure supply of energy. Security measures at home are made more difficult by the centralised and vulnerable structure of the production and distribution of energy.

Strategic inflexibility in the Middle East limits Western policy options

Doves see the Western military presence in Saudi Arabia as a provocation to Muslim opinion. Hawks realise that the US economy would be hurt by war with all states in the Middle East that the US considers sponsor terrorism.

Before the attacks on the US, American and Western global strategy gave a very high priority to ensuring access to Middle East oil. This priority translates into a large investment of taxpayers' money, personnel, military equipment and political capital.

The cost of policing the Gulf since 1990 is hard to calculate accurately. However, the scale can be judged. If the regional policing cost were $100 billion it would, according to some estimates, add $14 to the price of a barrel of oil.[6] This is equivalent to some 30% of combined UK and US military expenditure.

The political cost to the West is also high. Western support for democratic values in the region is at best muted.

When traditional strategists look to 2020 or 2050, they still see Middle Eastern oil as the key issue in international energy policy. In the UK, this view informs the House of Commons investigation into Energy Security which assumes that we will have to import our energy. In the US, the now famous Hart–Rudman report on Homeland Defense takes the same approach as does the US Joint Chiefs of Staff Strategy document 'Joint Vision 2020', published in January 2002. September 11th has begun affecting US energy policy. In addition to a boost in domestic oil production there is for the first time support for fuel cells to run cars.[7]

Vulnerability of production and transportation of energy supplies to terrorist attack

One way to substitute or supplement Middle-Eastern oil supplies is to increase oil and gas production in other regions of the world. This can be a short-term fix. However the world already faces a shortfall of supplies around 2020, so increasing production now will only bring this date closer.

Increasing nuclear power brings with it its own strategic problems. The author drew attention to strategic vulnerability created in any nation by the building of nuclear reactors in a 1989 study.[8] As long ago as 1976 the Royal Commission on Environmental Pollution had noted that large areas of Europe would still be contaminated with cesium had nuclear power been in use during the Second World War.

Since September 11th there has been concern about the physical protection of nuclear power plants. France has publicly deployed point air-defence systems around Cap de la Hague. However the initiative will continue to lie with the terrorist who has a number of means of attack.

Rather than construction of more nuclear reactors, attention should be given to protection of those that do exist and options for phasing out their use. Recent studies and conferences have drawn attention to these problems and have called for greater concern from governments.[9]

Centralised conventional electricity production and oil refining are vulnerable as well. In a September 19th letter to US senators, three former senior officials in US Republican and Democratic administrations wrote, 'It is not enough just to ensure uninterruptible supplies of transportation fuels and electricity, given the vulnerability of refiners, pipelines and the electricity grid to military and terrorist attacks.'[10]

Truck bombs or rocket-propelled grenades directed at oil refineries and chemical plants could produce devastating effects. Major natural gas containers have a potential detonating power equal to nuclear weapons.

The three officials – R. James Woolsey, head of the Central Intelligence Agency during the Clinton administration, Admiral Thomas Moore, chairman of the Joint Chiefs of Staff for President Richard Nixon, and Robert McFarlane, national security adviser during the Reagan administration – recommend government action to encourage the development of renewable energy resources.

In addition to the problems of energy supplies inside a country there is the additional vulnerability of sea transportation. Tankers carrying oil and natural gas are potential bombs. Hijacking tankers at sea is an obvious next step for people wishing to carry out mass attacks. Piracy may become a new form of strategic attack.

The way ahead

Renewable energy and energy efficiency offer a financially viable solution to the twin strategic issues of dependency on Middle-Eastern oil and the vulnerability of domestic nuclear and conventional energy production and distribution facilities.

The vast majority of oil production, some 95%, is devoted to transportation requirements. The technical solution is to change from internal combustion engines to hybrid and fuel-cell technology. In his 2000 election campaign Vice President Al Gore produced a plan to eliminate the internal combustion engine over a quarter of a century. Stankovic[11] has argued that the same objective could be achieved in ten years. Many vehicle production companies have produced prototype and production vehicles using both hybrid petrol/fuel-cell engines and pure hybrids using hydrogen as the power supply. Some also use electric power.

International leadership is necessary to manage so large a change in industrial infrastructure. The key is for governments to lead by announcing that their own fleet purchases of vehicles will use new engine types from a set target date, say five years hence, and co-ordinate such a decision with other purchasers and suppliers.

Some leading oil producers such as Shell and BP have already begun to plan for a transition away from oil as an energy source by mid-century because they recognise the dwindling supply and the growing policy imperative of reducing environmental impact. This transition from nineteenth-century to twenty-first-century technology should be speeded up.

The provision of electric power supply is highly concentrated, as the three former officials have observed. In their letter they recommended that: 'disbursed, renewable and domestic supplies of fuels and electricity, such as energy produced naturally from wind, solar, geothermal, incremental hydro, and agricultural biomass', would solve the problem of the vulnerability of infrastructure.

Three per cent of wind resources could provide 30% of global energy needs. Solar power has similar potential.

At present the industrialised world obtains just 7% of its energy supplies from renewable sources. The bulk of this is from hydroelectric power. Wind power is advanced in some states. In Denmark, it provides 14%, projected to rise to 30% in a few years' time. The capital cost of wind power is similar to fossil fuel and cheaper than nuclear.

Recommended measure:

☐ **A transition strategy to renewable energy should be the focus of attention for the leading industrialised nations of the G-8, beginning at the coming meeting in Canada.**

Weapons of mass destruction

The September 11th attacks, the US response, the India–Pakistan conflict and the anthrax attacks have created concerns about the use of weapons of mass destruction. Will future terrorist attacks include nuclear, chemical or biological weapons? Will there be a nuclear response from the US? Will another nuclear power be attacked, such as Russia? Will there be a nuclear war over Kashmir? All these problems raise the larger issue of what should be done about weapons of mass destruction.

Weapons of mass destruction come in three types: nuclear, biological and chemical. All three can be fitted to many types of what the military call 'delivery systems', which include missiles, aircraft, vehicles and maritime vessels. Nuclear weapons have been preferred to chemical and biological weapons because they destroy things as well as people and because they are more reliable. Strictly speaking, chemical and biological weapons do not actually 'destroy' anything. Even the people they kill are not destroyed since the corpses remain.

No countries admit to having chemical or biological weapons, though some states, mainly in the Middle East, are believed to have them. Countries without any weapons of mass destruction want them all to be eliminated through verifiable and enforceable treaties. Chemical and biological weapons are banned under separate conventions. The chemical weapons ban is supported by 145 states and has a verification and enforcement mechanism. The biological ban has neither. There is no convention banning nuclear weapons.

China, France, Russia, the UK and the US have for many years publicly acknowledged having nuclear weapons. The US and Russia still possess tens of thousands of weapons, more than 90% of the world's stockpile. Belgium, Germany, Greece, Italy, the Netherlands and Turkey all have arrangements through NATO to use US nuclear weapons in wartime. Israel has had nuclear weapons since the 1960s, India tested one in 1974 and India and Pakistan announced that they had made them in 1998. Some industrialised states such as Japan and Germany could make them if they chose to. Some countries, including Taiwan, South Korea, Argentina,

Brazil and Sweden, abandoned nuclear-weapons programmes before they made the bomb. South Africa, Belarus, Ukraine and Khazakstan unilaterally disarmed. Others including Iran, Iraq and North Korea are thought to be trying to acquire them.

The five traditional nuclear-armed states have all agreed in principle to nuclear disarmament under the nuclear Non-Proliferation Treaty but they all state that nuclear weapons are the guarantee of their own security. They all encourage other nations not to acquire nuclear weapons, but this amounts to: 'Do as I say, not as I do.'

Potential use of weapons of mass destruction by Al Qaeda or other groups

The attacks of September 11th and the subsequent anthrax attacks turned the possibility of this type of action on the part of a non-governmental group into a source of real anxiety for many people. Until then, the conventional wisdom in governments was that this type of attack was unlikely because terrorists did not wish totally to alienate public opinion. Today it is clear that these attackers are not worried about public opinion and would destroy the societies they oppose if they could. The concern is that they and other groups may have the means to do so.

As long ago as 1979, Howard Moreland published how he had dsicovered the existing techniques for building a hydrogen bomb. Far simpler technology for building a Hiroshima-type atomic weapon has been in the public domain for years. A modern machine-engineering shop and a supply of uranium 235 are the main requirements.

The US now has well-established programmes to provide Russia with financial assistance to prevent nuclear materials getting into the hands of other countries and terrorists. Parallel programmes pay Russian nuclear scientists to work in civil programmes as an incentive against working abroad for such interests. Leading US specialists argue that these programmes need to be reinforced and a leading US Senator, Dick Lugar, has argued for making the programme global.[12]

Secret production of chemical and biological weapons is also a serious problem. One reason the US opposes a UN verification regime for biological weapons is because the administration considers the task impossible, and fears UN inspectors who are from other states would steal US biotechnology secrets.

Before September 11th there was already a considerable literature about the problem of independent groups and so-called 'rogue states' obtaining access to various types of weapons of mass destruction. There are sources all over the world. For example, the post-Soviet stocks of nuclear, chemical and biological weapons give rise to the most serious international concern. Military stocks and industrial facilities in many other states are also important sources.

There is much debate about how independent groups have in the past and may in the future gain access to these materials. Finding out this information has been a key objective of intelligence agencies as well as in the broader world of journalists and academics. As discussed before, international intelligence can only be effective against an international threat in an environment of international co-operation.

There are international inspections of civilian nuclear materials but none of military nuclear materials and none of biological agents. The Chemical Weapons Convention can be used to look at government and private activities. Such checks could be useful in ensuring that states not in the Treaty are isolated from the sources and in detecting whether or not guerrillas or individuals were acquiring them. These issues are discussed in the arms control and disarmament section below.

Potential use of nuclear weapons by the US

Use of nuclear weapons in the present conflict has been considered by the US but the possibility should not be exaggerated. President Bush may have considered using nuclear weapons on September 11th and shortly afterwards. Some officials in his government have privately expressed that view. The National Security Council considered the question in mid-September and ruled it out for the time being.

It still remains unclear why President Bush flew to the Headquarters of Strategic Command on September 11th. This command post at Offutt Air Force base in Nebraska controls US nuclear weapons in peacetime. It has little other purpose. It was a priority target in Cold War scenarios with Russia and is consequently not a likely place to take the president as part of some long-standing emergency plan. On the other hand, he may have gone there precisely because it was an unlikely place to go to and has good communications.

Much has yet to be clarified about the US response in those first days. For example, why has Vice President Dick Cheney apparently been removed from his position of influence since mid-September? Keeping him in apparent isolation for so long on security grounds is one explanation, but scarcely adequate for a person of such influence. Why was the Secretary of State Colin Powell unable to speak to the President for ten hours after the WTC attacks? Was this because of major disagreements about the best way to retaliate? Nuclear options against terrorists are discussed in official US publications.[13]

In a recent speech, Britain's top military officer warned of the danger that the United States might respond to further attacks by giving in to: 'The desire to use greater force with less constraints, less distinction and less proportionality – something that strikes at the acceptable laws of armed conflict, and exposes our centre of strategic gravity [our will] by radicalising the opinion of the Islamic world in favour of Al Qaeda.'

It is unclear if he was talking about a mass conventional attack such as World War Two-style bombing of cities or referring to nuclear weapons. This kind of language is often a deliberately ambiguous reference to nuclear weapons.

Nuclear weapons in India and Pakistan

India and Pakistan have been working on building nuclear weapons, and ballistic missiles to carry them, for many years. Both states exploded several weapons in underground tests in 1998. One response of the US to the September 11th attacks was to lift a ban on military exports to the two countries imposed after the nuclear tests, in order to gain political support for its operations in Afghanistan. There is pressure from UK arms companies to increase exports to these states.

A nuclear war between India and Pakistan looks more likely than on any previous occasion. The Indian defence minister has even explained that he thinks India could survive a nuclear attack and go on and win a nuclear war. With several dozen nuclear weapons on each side and an Indian population of around one billion people, he may turn out to be right. Yet the horror induced by a 'victory' of this kind, with vast amounts of casualties and nuclear contamination, could lead to an effective ban on all such weapons. On the other hand, states could react in the traditional manner of building more weapons to win the next war.

Strategies for responding to the threats from weapons of mass destruction

There are three main strategies for dealing with weapons of mass destruction. One approach involves the use or threat of use of force, the second focuses on the control and elimination of these weapons, the third is civil defence to reduce their impact. For most of the last fifty years, the first two active strategies have been used together, sometimes in contradiction, sometimes in mutual support.

Most people hold the view that weapons of mass destruction exist as a deterrent and will never be used, and that our governments are doing what they can to get them banned. The deterrent idea is mostly thought to mean that the threat of their use in retaliation is enough to stop anyone from using them. In reality the nations with nuclear weapons have always been prepared to use them for fighting and winning, much like any other major war, though many people operating those policies have privately considered them foolish.

Missile 'defences' combined with other weapons are intended to allow the US to wage nuclear war on China or Russia without sustaining casualties, as has already been managed in conventional conflicts in Iraq, Kosovo and Afghanistan.

Deterrence, war and missile 'defence'

Deterrence has been central to US and NATO military and political planning for fifty years. Its supporters believe that it prevented war with the Soviet Union. However, deterrence and indeed war depend on having someone to shoot at. The problem with guerrilla groups with suicide fighters is that they are not deterred and they do not present a target. In tackling such independent groups our own weapons are irrelevant. The only useful strategy is prevention.

Another problem with deterrence is that it allows the comfortable delusion to arise that we can have weapons but never have to use them. How many youths have found themselves in the dock explaining that they only went out with a knife or gun as a deterrent? 'I never meant to use it . . . '

In the Cold War, a circular argument was used to justify more weapons. It was acknowledged that if a deterrent is so terrible that no one will ever use it, it lacks credibility and therefore more usable deterrents are needed. In a climate of secrecy and paranoia the Soviet Union and US-led NATO built all sorts of nuclear weapons, including Hiroshima-size bombs that could be fired from artillery guns and bombs carried by helicopters for destroying submarines. Weapons became faster and more accurate, more capable, more of a deterrent. In short, the more dangerous things are, the safer we are.

The terms deterrence, war fighting and defences often get confused. In particular, the word 'deterrence' is used to describe many different ideas and weapons. This has best been explained by the general who commanded US nuclear forces for President George Bush Senior and who was responsible for developing nuclear options during the Gulf War. He remarked in a speech criticising deterrence that:[14]

'As nuclear weapons and actors multiplied, deterrence took on too many names, too many roles, overreaching an already extreme strategic task. Surely nuclear weapons summoned great caution in superpower relationships . . . The exorbitant price of nuclear war quickly exceeded the rapidly depreciating value of a tenuous mutual wariness. Invoking deterrence became a cheap rhetorical parlor trick, a verbal sleight of hand. Proponents persist in dressing it up to court changing times and temperaments, hemming and re-hemming to fit shrinking or distorted threats . . . It gives easy semantic cover to nuclear weapons, masking the horrors of employment with siren veils of infallibility . . . How is it that we subscribed to a strategy that required near perfect understanding of an enemy from whom we were deeply alienated and largely isolated? . . . **Deterrence was a dialogue of the blind with the deaf. In the final analysis, it was largely a bargain we in the West made with ourselves** [emphasis added]. At best it is a gamble no mortal should pretend to make. At worst it invokes death on a scale rivalling the power of the creator.'

Nevertheless, in a formal statement of US national policy, the general commanding US nuclear forces explained that, with respect to Russia,[15] 'stability equates to parity in war-fighting capability'. The US's war-fighting strategy is explicit and formalised in Major Attack Option 1 of the Single Integrated Operating Plan (SIOP MAO1) for the use of US nuclear weapons.[16] This plan is designed to destroy Russian and Chinese weapons before they can be launched. The strategy is often called counterforce or first strike or first use because it involves countering the other side's forces by striking first.

The Anti-Ballistic Missile Treaty of 1972 prevented the US and Russia from developing comprehensive systems for shooting down long-range missiles. This treaty banning such anti-missile missiles was signed after the US persuaded the Soviets that without such a ban there would be an even greater uncontrollable arms race between missiles, anti-missile missiles and anti-anti-missile missiles. This is why the ABM Treaty is described as a basis of strategic stability.

US and Russian nuclear weapons are designed to be accurate enough to target the other side's weapons. The Russian arsenal was always technically inferior to the American. The Russian arsenal has deteriorated and the US has kept its in prime condition. Two thousand US nuclear warheads kept ready to fire are more than enough to overwhelm Russian and Chinese forces, even allowing for several warheads per target and leaving out the US conventional smart weapons. The US has further nuclear weapons available.

Even in Britain, with a force of a couple of hundred nuclear weapons, a so-called sub-strategic version of Trident has been built for contingencies other than retaliation after the nation has been destroyed, when deterrence would have failed. The US, other NATO nations and Russia all reserve the legal right to start a nuclear war.

The incoming Bush team supported strengthening the counterforce approach. Several of the people the president has now appointed to key positions described how counterforce supported by missile 'defence' and unconstrained by treaties should be the new administration's policy.[17]

The latest planning is intended to fulfil this goal. The president's nuclear review announced in January 2002 plans to take some warheads off their missiles, rather like taking the bullets from a gun, but will keep more than enough to implement option one of the Single Integrated Operating Plan. In addition, the intention is to be able to test new nuclear weapons within six months. New weapons may be built designed to destroy very difficult targets like bunkers.

The US is spending large amounts of money on non-nuclear weapons designed to negate opposition missiles and satellites. Building on present US supremacy, the Bush administration is now determined to build up a full range of missile shields not only targeted at incoming missiles but also at non-US satellites. Satellites are becoming ever more important in civilian and military communications and in electronic eavesdropping, satellite photography and remote sensing of the atmosphere. In fact, the proposed lasers in space – which may be tested in a few years' time – will be far more effective against these satellites than against enemy rockets. In the language of US Space Command, lasers are weapons for dominating the full spectrum of conflict. Increasing numbers of states are launching satellites or buying satellites that other states launch.

A clearer picture of the implication of missile 'defences' emerges when these defence systems are considered in the context of how a war with a 'rogue state' might be fought. For example, if the US ever went to war in Korea, the US army and air force would fight alongside their South Korean partners with strong support from the US Pacific fleet, the Marines, and US-based air power. Missile 'defence' would be there to pick off any missiles that survived US conventional or nuclear strikes. Missile 'defence' is to be used as part of fighting wars, not just as a defensive shield.

Another example of the planned offensive use of missile 'defence' is in combination with smart conventional weapons. US security planners have long sought to give the president an option to win a nuclear war without tossing the entire planet into the incinerator of a nuclear holocaust. What better way than to use smart conventional weapons to destroy the other side's nukes? The Clinton administration spent some energy working this out and even tested the navy's Trident missiles with conventional warheads. US conventional weapons could destroy Russia and China's nuclear arsenals today. China's force is small but even Russia's four hundred or so nuclear missile launchers might be overwhelmed by the thousands of conventionally armed cruise missiles and stealth bombers in the US arsenal. A few might survive and be used in retaliation. If they could be shot down by the proposed missile 'defences', the US would be able to make it impossible for Russia and China to retaliate without having to use its own nuclear weapons. The smart weapons Washington is developing to track and destroy command bunkers and mobile missiles like the Scud would also be useful for destroying Russian and Chinese targets. Some officials in Washington call this 'humane' deterrence.

Advocates of missile 'defences' usually discuss them as if they existed in a box by themselves; once they are examined in the context of other weapons, their use in offensive operations becomes easy to see. Indeed, historically offensive and defensive weapons have been used together in the attack. A common analogy is that defences add the shield to the sword, giving a great advantage to the man with both. Adding the shield did not stop the arms race or resolve conflict. Commentators who ignore the 'offence-defence' connection are either disingenuous or incompetent.

Everyone wants to be defended but the policy described above risks war, is certainly no defence and may lead to an arms race. Ambassador Evan Galbraith, Donald Rumsfeld's personal representative to NATO, believes that such an arms race may be no bad thing:[18]

> 'I know the detractors, many in this room, will undoubtedly continue to groan about the arms race. Don't start an arms race. I might add we won the last one and I think that probably wasn't a bad idea.'

Galbraith was for many years chairman of the *National Review* – a very conservative and influential US journal whose support was important to Governor Bush's successful candidacy.

There are a number of other arguments for and against missile 'defence' aside from its use in offensive operations. One of the arguments in favour is that missile 'defences' are only intended for use in the case of so-called rogue nations, such as Libya, Iraq, North Korea and Syria. This is because they are so unpredictable and therefore unamenable to deterrence, and we should not be subject to blackmail by their weapons of mass destruction. These nations, however, only have small numbers of mostly short-range weapons, and these only travel around 500 km.[19] **'Rogue state' missiles all use the same engine design invented by Werner von Braun, which was used first in the Nazi V2, then in the Soviet Scud and most recently in North Korea's No Dong.** Ranges of around 1500 km have been achieved by placing one V2 engine on top of another in a second stage. While these ranges are adequate for Israel, Iran and the Arab states to threaten one another, when fired from Iran or Iraq they can barely reach the European Union let alone the United States. There is no major military industrial complex in 'rogue states' able to build these weapons. They would have to rely on supplies from Russia, China or NATO members.

The lack of any more powerful missile technology than the V2 is a testament to the success of non-proliferation efforts and an indication that the problem of missiles in the hands of 'rogue states' is exaggerated.

The term 'rogue state' is designed to convey the idea that these states are beyond reason. This is untrue. There have been succesful negotiations with North Korea and Iran. Saddam Hussein was a western ally until 1990. It is possible that the West would not have acted to remove Saddam Hussein from Kuwait if he had been known to have nuclear weapons or, as he in fact did have, chemical and biological weapons. It is more likely that in this case Israel and the US would have acted earlier. Advocates of missile 'defence' would be more convincing if they also supported arms control and engagement efforts.

The other argument in favour is that missile 'defences' are just to protect us from an accidental missile launch if deterrence fails. This is a fine idea by itself, but as we have seen they are designed to work with offensive weapons, and an adversary is unlikely to see it any other way.

One of the arguments against missile 'defence' is that it will cost too much, but if there is a good reason for having the weapons then it may be that the money would be well spent. In fact, the offensive nature of plans for missile 'defence' means that they are a poor idea, regardless of cost.

Another argument is that missile 'defence' will never work. Ted Postol of the Massachusetts Institute of Technology has argued that there are key problems with the essential physics involved – especially in trying to distinguish between real and fake incoming warheads.

Finally, there is an argument that missile 'defence' is inevitable and that Europeans should just ensure that it fits in with deterrence. This misses the point. The entire purpose of missile 'defence' is to prevent the 'other side' from being able to strike at all. Thus, we deter them but they do not deter us. People can call this deterrence if they want to. A more accurate word is domination.

Europeans who are prepared to endorse missile 'defences' should understand that this will involve placing US missile systems in Europe. These systems will necessarily include bases or ships for firing interceptor missiles, not only the radars that have attracted political attention at Fylingdales in Yorkshire and Thule in Greenland. **The US will want missile bases and not just radar stations in Europe because the flight paths of hypothetical missiles passing from the Middle East or Russia to the US pass over Europe.**

Weapons management and threat elimination

The second major approach to weapons of mass destruction is arms control and disarmament or, as I prefer to describe it (to get away from the language of the Cold War), weapons management and threat elimination.

Preventive strategies need to balance the openness in international co-operation required to prevent proliferation to new states and independent groups on the one hand, and on the other the secrecy needed to protect the state's own weapons. An international system controlling all nuclear, biological and chemical materials that can be used as weapons cannot come into being while states regard the possession of these materials themselves as essential to national security.

In the early 1960s, the Kennedy administration carried out an exhaustive internal analysis over whether to support more of its allies in the acquisition of nuclear weapons or to seek Soviet collaboration in restricting them. The subsequent Johnson administration launched a global campaign to restrict the number of nations with nuclear weapons. This campaign reached fruition in the 1970 nuclear Non-Proliferation Treaty.

Today all nations have signed the treaty except for Cuba, India, Israel and Pakistan. A few treaty members, who happen to be the permanent members of the UN Security Council (China, France, Russia, the United Kingdom and the United States), are allowed a temporary right to hold nuclear arms until nuclear disarmament can be agreed. NATO members reserve a controversial special right for their armed forces to use US nuclear weapons in wartime. Some train air forces to do this.

The NPT has proved effective in helping control the 'bad guys'. It provided the international legal framework according to which Iraq and North Korea have been held to account and Iran has been subject to regular inspection of its nuclear facilities. Inspections, combined with information from defectors, were used to uncover Iraq's secret biological, chemical and nuclear programmes and serve as a precedent for what can be achieved when there is an international consensus.

That consensus fell apart over the Palestinian issue and as US–Russian relations deteriorated in the 1990s. If the major powers keep their nuclear arms and act in a high-handed manner it is much more difficult to rally support against smaller nations, however badly run, who want to join the club.

The countries that agreed never to develop the bomb did so on the basis that those with it would disarm. In 2000, a consensus was reached among all the states party to the Non-Proliferation Treaty on a thirteen-point programme of action leading to nuclear disarmament. Britain, China, France, Russia and the US gave an 'unequivocal' undertaking to achieve nuclear disarmament. As yet none of them has even commissioned a study of how to do this.

Disarmament agreements can be effective. For example, the US–Soviet START treaty negotiated by Ronald Reagan and Mikhail Gorbachev saw many missiles and planes destroyed with comprehensive verification procedures.

Other negotiations have so far been fruitless. These include attempts to control military radioactive materials and ban weapons in space. The Bush administration has aborted a number of agreements that had almost reached fruition. These included the Comprehensive Test Ban Treaty, the second Strategic Arms Reduction Treaty and the Biological Weapons Convention verification protocol.

Effective measures taken at the end of the Cold War should serve as the basis for international agreements to control and eliminate nuclear and conventional weapons. In the days of Ronald Reagan, Mikhail Gorbachev and George Bush Senior, two other effective and verifiable treaties were signed. The first of these was the Intermediate Nuclear Forces Treaty (INF) which prohibited both the US and the Soviet Union (and now Russia, its successor state) from possessing any ballistic or cruise missiles fired from land with ranges between 500 and 5,500 km. Under the treaty hundreds of missiles were chopped up, but the nuclear warheads themselves were, at American insistence, excluded.

The second treaty governs conventional armed forces in Europe (CFE).

It provides for the destruction, control and verification of tens of thousands of tanks, armoured vehicles, artillery and aircraft throughout Europe. The conventional wisdom of the time was that the treaty was not workable because it required too much technical and political detail. This proved to be wrong. The application of political will meant that issues that academics had pondered for decades were resolved in days. This work should provide the basis for a global structure for disarmament. Unfortunately, there is no interest in proceeding along these lines, among either states or pressure groups.

It is essential to restrict conventional weapons as a means of restricting conventional war and limiting the spread of weapons of mass destruction. A lesson of the Gulf War was not to fight the US unless you have nuclear arms, the head of the Indian armed forces remarked at the time. In 1993, the then Secretary of Defence in the US government, the late Les Aspin, expressed a similar view. He pointed out that Third World nations would seek to use weapons of mass destruction to counterbalance US conventional might. Therefore, a strong initiative based on the framework of the INF and CFE Treaties can serve as one part of a comprehensive effort towards threat elimination.

Such an initiative from within the West would be a considerable confidence-building measure for the weaker countries that seek weapons of mass destruction to counter US conventional supremacy.

Civil defence

In Britain this is co-ordinated in the Cabinet Office. Since the end of the Cold War much of the civil defence infrastructure has been closed or downgraded. Its ability to protect the public against nuclear attack had been rightly ridiculed. Since September 11th public bodies have reviewed their ability to respond. This effort is closely connected to the intelligence strategies to detect attacks before they are made. It is difficult to make a proper assessment of the effectiveness of these measures from outside government.

A difficult calculation is involved when considering devoting public resources to an event that may or may not happen but if it does will have a great impact. In general, the response would be the same as that to any major disaster but there is a range of scenarios. One of the most frightening is a large-scale biological attack. Clearly the fear induced by the anthrax letters in America vastly exceeded the actual impact, as only six people were killed. In general the medical profession is able to treat infectious diseases. One of the critical public-health issues is getting to outbreaks rapidly enough and with enough organisation to prevent further infection.

The way ahead

Tony Blair and George Bush have named weapons of mass destruction as the greatest threat to our societies and yet neither proposes any plan for eliminating the threat. While the US military budget alone is now $380 billion, the nations of the world cannot even find one thousandth of that to sustain the $330 million budget that the International Atomic Energy Agency needs to check up on nuclear materials. Its representative spoke at the UN in the aftermath of September 11th and complained, in the restrained style of international bureaucracy, that:[20]

> This review of some of the IAEA's activities makes it clear that the scope of our work continues to expand. In the environment of zero real growth budgets, to which the agency has been subjected for over a decade, some of these priorities cannot be accommodated. The compromises achieved to date to resolve near-term budget issues should not be mistaken for long-term solutions. If the agency is to fulfil its mandate while maintaining the required balance among its priority activities, we must find better ways to ensure adequate and predictable funding. We must also have the foresight, when planning our activities, to invest in preventive measures rather than simply responding to crises – when it is often too late and much more costly.

Looking ahead into the middle of the century, where do current trends with weapons of mass destruction take us? A number of possible futures present themselves. One is where US hegemony presides over a relatively stable state of armaments and where potential adversaries have been either cajoled or bombed into acquiescence. Another is one where there is sporadic use of weapons of mass destruction in Western cities and between Third World nations and nations seek succour in missiles and anti-missile systems. Japan and the European Union develop their own nuclear weapons. We learn to live with it.

Then again, there may yet be global holocaust. The fear of attacking for fear of retaliation – the so-called deterrence theory – has always been risky and in this scenario fails, given a less and less rational and predictable world. A major world war breaks out in which hundreds of millions are killed while the follow-on economic and environmental impact threatens the survival of humanity itself. Nuclear arms, genetically engineered biological weapons and weapons yet to be thought of combine to produce world war, with consequences that defy the imagination. It is easy to forget that in 1914 there has been no war in Europe between the great powers since 1870 and many people thought it impossible.

In all of these scenarios, the global village takes a beating. Whole blocks are burnt out. With no police and no gun control, village life as we know it becomes a thing of the past.

There is a brighter, less defeatest vision, in which every effort is made to eliminate the threat of weapons of mass destruction and to limit all other forms of armaments. War becomes as unthinkable as it is today between Germany, France and Britain. Civil wars are much reduced.

At this time of serious destabilisation of international security, it is necessary to create a different and positive dynamic. Governments and pressure groups alike should adopt as comprehensive an approach to weapons management and elimination as that used for military planning. The approach should aim to build on coalitions of like-minded states and draw in the US, Russia, China and other major powers, through the UN system when possible. **The European Union should become a world leader in weapons management and elimination. This would be a more useful means of countering the negative aspects of US policy than trying to compete militarily.**

There needs to be a combination of short- and long-term measures, with preliminary work begun immediately to enable the larger longer-term objectives to reach fruition.

Recommended measures:

❑ **The following programme should provide the political context for weapons of mass destruction in South Asia and other areas of regional proliferation.**

❑ **The UK and like-minded states should implement the provisions of the biological weapons verification protocol. This would make it harder for guerrilla groups to gain access to these materials and enable future detection efforts to 'eliminate potential suspects from their enquiries', so saving time and increasing confidence, experience and political momentum.**

❑ **Increase funding for the nuclear inspectorate of the International Atomic Energy Agency.**

❑ **Implement the agreement made in 2000 at the Non Proliferation Treaty review conference[21] on a thirteen-point programme. The House of Commons should initiate a joint Defence and Foreign Affairs Committee investigation of this programme. The short-term**

British contribution should be to remove the warheads from Trident and put them in storage. The Trident submarines would still be exercised at sea. This measure was turned down in the Strategic Defence Review in 1997 because sending the submarines to sea would send too strong a signal. This is a strange argument as normally deterrence is described as being all about signals.

- ❏ NPT implementation should involve the timed and phased elimination of nuclear weapons by 2020.
- ❏ A combined verification and enforcement regime for nuclear, chemical and biological weapons should be developed.
- ❏ Initiate a programme to control and eliminate conventional weapons, building on the provisions of the INF and CFE Treaties and covering naval vessels, with the objective of a verified halt to the production and trade in such weapons by 2010 and the elimination of most major weapon systems by 2020.
- ❏ No new military production contracts should be made after 2010.
- ❏ The UK and other European states should not participate in the US missile 'defence' programmes and should base their opposition on the offensive nature of these systems. At a minimum, support should be linked to full implementation of the NPT and other arms control regimes by all states including the USA.

Conclusion

The proposals sketched out in this paper are intended to provide a practical and multi-dimensional route to a less threatening, more just world. It is easy to feel overwhelmed in the face of terrorism, rogue states and a rogue superpower. The agreements made at the end of the Cold War demonstrate that Ronald Reagan's motto 'trust but verify' can be turned into effective politics and that seemingly insurmountable political and technical problems can be overcome providing that there is political will.

That will can come from us. The international demonstrations of the 1980s provided a brake on the momentum of the arms race. Without that movement, I have little doubt that the world would have fallen into the nuclear abyss. More recently international pressure helped bring change to South Africa and created the land-mines convention. As the world changes, we have to struggle to adapt our thinking. Are our challenges any greater than those faced by people in earlier generations? I doubt it.

We need to re-engage Americans because of their leading role in the world, rather than criticising from the sidelines. The Internet provides a powerful tool. Rather than keeping our concerns over US policy to ourselves, we should use the Internet to talk to Americans directly. We will find the experience instructive.

Talking about peace and disarmament is sometimes thought of as unrealistic and for idealists only, so it's interesting to realise who said the following: **'All the nations of the world, for realistic as well spiritual reasons, must come to the abandonment of the use of force'**. This statement comes not from a pacifist pamphlet, but from a short communiqué called the Atlantic Charter[22] issued by Winston Churchill and Franklin Roosevelt at their first wartime meeting. This was in August 1941 aboard HMS *Prince of Wales* recently repaired after fighting the *Bismarck*. Their statement looked forward to a postwar world of free trade and democracy with the arms industry much diminished.

They had much else on their minds at the time. Human civilisation was at its lowest ebb. The Soviet Union was expected to surrender to Hitler in the face of the Nazi attack. This would have enabled him to turn his full attention on Britain that autumn. America was not yet in the war. Yet, these leaders saw the need to spell out an agenda worth fighting for. They understood even before the invention of nuclear weapons that a civilisation without an international system was doomed to destroy itself. Who are we to aim for anything less?

Summary of Recommendations

A transition strategy to renewable energy should be the focus of attention for the leading industrialised nations of the G-8, beginning at the coming meeting in Canada. 28

The following programme should provide the political context for weapons of mass destruction in South Asia and other areas of regional proliferation. 41

The UK and like-minded states should implement the provisions of the biological weapons verification protocol. This would make it harder for guerrilla groups to gain access to these materials and enable future detection efforts to 'eliminate potential suspects from their enquiries', so saving time and increasing confidence, experience and political momentum. 41

Increase funding for the nuclear inspectorate of the International Atomic Energy Agency. 41

Implement the agreement made in 2000 at the Non Proliferation Treaty review conference[21] on a thirteen-point programme. The House of Commons should initiate a joint Defence and Foreign Affairs Committee investigation of this programme. The short-term British contribution should be to remove the warheads from Trident and put them in storage. The Trident submarines would still be exercised at sea. This measure was turned down in the Strategic Defence Review in 1997 because sending the submarines to sea would send too strong a signal. This is a strange argument as normally deterrence is described as being all about signals. 41

NPT implementation should involve the timed and phased elimination of nuclear weapons by 2020. 42

A combined verification and enforcement regime for nuclear, chemical and biological weapons should be developed. 42

Initiate a programme to control and eliminate conventional weapons, building on the provisions of the INF and CFE Treaties and covering naval vessels, with the objective of a verified halt to the production and trade in such weapons by 2010 and the elimination of most major weapon systems by 2020. 42

No new military production contracts should be made after 2010. 42

The UK and other European states should not participate in the US missile 'defence' programmes and should base their opposition on the offensive nature of these systems. At a minimum, support should be linked to full implementation of the NPT and other arms control regimes by all states including the USA. 42

References

1 http://www.iaea.org/worldatom/Press/P_release/2001/
   nt_pressrelease.shtml
2 www.stimson.org
3 www.undcp.org
4 *The Grand Chessboard – American Primacy and Its Geostrategic Imperatives*,
   Zbigniew Brzezinski, Basic Books, 1997, p. 40
5 *Intelligence Services in the Information Age*, Michael Herman, Cass, 2001, p. 231
6 Sinisa Stankovic, BDSP partnership presentation at the *Guardian*/RUSI
   conference, 30 October 2001
7 www.whitehouse.gov
8 *Nuclear Minefield: Nuclear and Chemical Plants in Conventional War in Europe*,
   British–American Security Information Council, 1990
9 www.iaea.int and www.nci.org
10 *Inside EPA*, Vol. 22, No. 40, 5 October 2001, Inside Washington
   Publishers, via InsideEPA.com
11 Stankovic, op. cit.
12 www.ransac.org
13 Joint Chiefs of Staff, Joint Doctrine, JP, 12 March 2001
14 General Lee Butler's remarks at the National Press Club, 2 February 1998,
   'The Risks of Deterrence: From Superpowers to Rogue Leaders',
   www.cdi.org
15 Admiral Richard W. Meiss, Senate Armed Services Committee Hearings
   on FY 2000 Defense Authorization Act, Part 7, p. 365, 14 April 1999
16 Natural Resources Defence Council study on the nuclear war plan,
   www.nrdc.org
17 www.nipp.org
18 Ambassador Evan Galbraith, speech at the Royal United Services Institute,
   November 2001
19 'European Missile Defence and the Potential Ballistic Missile Risk'. Lt-
   Col Cees Wolterbeek, Weapons of Mass Destruction Centre, NATO HQ,
   July 2001
20 http://f40.iaea.org/worldatom/PressStatements/2001/ebsp2001
   no10.shtml
21 www.reachingcriticalwill.org, www.acronym.org www.basicint.org
22 www.nato.int. NATO Basic Documents